To:
_____

From:
_____

Date:
_____

Think of GOOD THINGS

Written by Rochelle St. John Ruiz • Illustrated by Pennie Mirande

Copyright © 2021 (Second Edition) Rochelle St. John Ruiz
Copyright © 2017 (First Edition) Rochelle St. John Ruiz

THINK OF GOOD THINGS

Written by Rochelle St. John Ruiz
Illustrated by Pennie Mirande

ISBN 9780578838960

All rights reserved solely by the author. The author guarantees all contents are orginal and do not infringe upon the legal rights of any other person or work. No part of this book may be reproduced in any form without the permission of the author.

Unless otherwise noted, Scripture quotations taken from the HOLY BIBLE NEW INTERNATIONAL VERSION (NIV) Copyright © 1973, 1978, 1984, 2011 by Biblica, Inc.® Used by permission. All rights reserved worldwide.

www.rochellestjohnruiz.com

Additional graphic design and typesetting by Liza DeYounge

Printed in China

To my husband, John Paul, and our inspiring daughters, Brianna and Matteya - you are three of the most beautiful and incredibly GOOD things in my life. I love you!
R.S.R.

To Daniel, Alex, and Trevor - you amaze me. I love being your mom! And to Drew - thanks for sharing your great grin.
P.M.

Whenever I feel a bit afraid and I don't know what to do or say,

Rainbows in the sky -
I love the colors they display.

Sitting on a beach
and watching **seagulls** as they play.

Whenever I feel a bit afraid
and I don't know what to do or say,

I think of **GOOD** things
and then I don't feel so afraid.

Shooting

stars

at

night

can make my worries disappear.

Tulips in the spring
remind me miracles are real.

Worshiping the Lord and really knowing that **He's near.**

Whenever I feel a bit afraid
and I don't know what
to do or say,

I think of **GOOD THINGS**
and then I don't feel so afraid.

Sometimes there are things
that make us scared within,
it doesn't matter if we're
old or young;

But if we make the choice to think about **GOOD THINGS**, we soon will notice that our fears are gone!

Playing in the snow
with
snowflakes
twinkling
all
around.

Playing on the bars —
the best is hanging
upside down!

Running

in a

field

of corn

that's

higher

than

my head!

Getting a

BIG HUG

when it is time

to go to bed.

Whenever I feel a bit afraid and I don't know what to do or say,

I think of **GOOD THINGS** and then I don't feel so afraid.

I think of **GOOD THINGS** and then I don't feel so afraid.

"**Whatever** is true, whatever is noble,
whatever is right,
whatever is pure, whatever is lovely,
whatever is admirable -
if anything is excellent or praiseworthy -
think about such things."

- Philippians 4:8 NIV

Can you find these things?

-The little boy's red blanket on every page
-All four seasons: winter, spring, summer, and fall
-The beach ball - 4 times
-The author's two daughters holding hands

Can you answer these questions?

How many times do we see the little boy on his bed the night he wore his green pajamas?

What happened to the little boy when he chose to think about good things?

Did you notice that the window reflected the good things the boy was thinking about?

How did the window change from the beginning of the book to the end?

Are all the boy's good thoughts in the window on the last page?

What are some GOOD things YOU like to think of?